THE FLETCHER SCHOOL OF LAW AND DIPLOMACY
A Graduate School of International Affairs
Administered with the Cooperation of Harvard University
TUFTS UNIVERSITY · MEDFORD, MASSACHUSETTS

The Diplomacy
of Economic Development

THE WILLIAM L. CLAYTON LECTURES
ON INTERNATIONAL ECONOMIC AFFAIRS
AND FOREIGN POLICY

CLAYTON LECTURES

POWER AND DIPLOMACY
> Dean Acheson (1957–1958)

DIPLOMACY IN THE NUCLEAR AGE
> Lester B. Pearson (1958–1959)

THE DIPLOMACY OF ECONOMIC DEVELOPMENT
> Eugene R. Black (1959–1960)

The Diplomacy of
Economic Development

Eugene R. Black

With a foreword by
CHRISTIAN A. HERTER

HARVARD UNIVERSITY PRESS · *Cambridge, Massachusetts* · *1961*

Distributed in Great Britain by Oxford University Press, London

Library of Congress Catalog Card Number 60-15888

Printed in the United States of America

THE WILLIAM L. CLAYTON LECTURES

The William L. Clayton Center for International Economic Affairs was established in 1952 at the Fletcher School of Law and Diplomacy, Tufts University, in honor and recognition of Mr. Clayton's services as one of the country's leading business-statesmen and its first Under Secretary of State for Economic Affairs. Mr. Clayton is founder and retired head of Anderson, Clayton & Company, the world's largest cotton merchants. His public service includes the following offices: Assistant Secretary of Commerce, 1942–44; Administrator of the Surplus War Property Administration; Assistant Secretary of State, 1944–46; and Under Secretary of State for Economic Affairs, 1946–48.

The foundation of the William L. Clayton Center was officially sponsored by the American Cotton Shippers Association, honoring "the accomplishments of Mr. Clayton both in the international cotton trade and as a public servant in the field of economic diplomacy," and "as a means of recognizing his substantial service to the Nation and extending the influence of his example in the field of international trade and diplomacy." Some two hundred individuals, business firms, banks, and foundations — principally connected with the cotton trade — joined in contributing the endowment for the Clayton Center.

The program of the Clayton Center — devoted to education and research — includes the William L. Clayton Professorship of International Economic Affairs, a program of research and current policy studies, a program of Clayton Fellowships to encourage and assist outstanding young men and women to prepare for careers in international economic affairs and diplomacy, and the annual Clayton Lectures by persons distinguished in the field of diplomacy, trade, or scholarship in international affairs. The Clayton Lectures were inaugurated by former Secretary of State Dean Acheson, in October 1957, which also marked the twenty-fifth year of the Fletcher School of Law and Diplomacy.

Contents

THE CLAYTON LECTURES

Foreword

EUGENE BLACK's book, *The Diplomacy of Economic Development*, is a valuable addition to the growing literature on this subject. In it can be found observations, insights, and conclusions by one of the major practitioners of two arts — neither diplomacy nor economics yet being precise sciences — of paramount concern to the entire world.

I am in agreement with Mr. Black's emphasis on the need for that kind of economic planning which seeks to provide flexible, sensible, alternative choices for policy-makers rather than to establish an unyielding mold into which a society must be forced in order that economic objectives may be achieved.

Of particular value is the observation that economic development is not an end in itself. If the process of development does not provide more hope and more opportunity for an ever-increasing number of persons, then the process is not successful from our point of view. Furthermore, the methods by which economic growth are achieved are at least as important as the growth itself. This, of course, is one of the major differences between the Sino-Soviet system and the great variety of economic systems in the free world.

Implicit in Mr. Black's book is the belief that the only

ix

really meaningful results of economic development are increases in the well-being — political and spiritual as well as economic — of individual citizens. Inasmuch as this well-being is the major concern of free and independent governments, it provides the basis for that meeting of the minds which is essential to free world partnerships. It is upon such mutuality of interests that nations can work together for progress and for peace.

Eugene Black is in a unique position to have expressed himself as he has in this book. His experience and his contacts with most of the leading figures of the world, both in the political and in the financial fields, give him a breadth of outlook possessed by few individuals. There is no need for me to recount in this brief foreword the contributions which he has made to the world's economic development through the World Bank, but I can say that through his grasp of basic problems, and his approach to fiscal responsibilities in their relation to these problems, he has performed one of those feats which leave their mark in the history of an era. In this period of rapid change, few people take the time to evaluate the beneficial impact of such institutions as the World Bank or to wonder where the world's process of economic growth would now stand had this agency and its dedicated officers not existed. One of the elements for optimism in the world today is that a man of Mr. Black's caliber is in a position to contribute so significantly in the field which he discusses in this book.

CHRISTIAN A. HERTER

The Clayton Lectures

Enlightenment
and Development

Few subjects have received more intensive study in recent years than the subject of economic development. The disciplines of all the social sciences have been brought to bear, and a whole new body of literature has resulted. To digest and order this body of literature would require a philosopher, well-schooled in academic economics, with a good command of history, who held a degree in civil engineering, with geography and anthropology as minor subjects, and who had taken a postgraduate course in modern social psychology.

Lacking these professional requirements, I cannot claim to make any analytical contributions to this sprawling subject. Analysis is the business of the scholar, and bankers are not normally scholars. As the president of an independent international development organization made up of sixty-eight sovereign nations, I am concerned with what might be called the diplomacy of economic development— that is, with how to secure advantages in terms of development without arousing too much hostility. Since the first requirement for economic development is change, and since change never comes easy, this is a delicate and often dangerous task.

While development diplomacy can operate between any two nations, its importance today lies in the relations between the materially rich countries and the materially poor countries of the world. But the adjectives "rich" and "poor" are much too vague to provide a useful ground for discussion. Professor Rostow, in his stimulating book, *The Stages of Economic Growth* (1960) has provided the analyst with a provocative way of describing nations from the point of view of development. For my purposes I will choose a simpler means, fully realizing that the dividing lines I will set out are arbitrary and probably serve no other purpose than my own.

In one part of the world I will lump together the countries of North America and Europe—including the Communist countries—and the older dominions of the British Commonwealth. Here the conditions and laws affecting the production, distribution, and consumption of wealth are more or less sufficient to make possible the growth of "affluent societies." Some, like theNorth American countries and most Western Europe, are enjoying what Professor Rostow calls "the age of high mass consumption"; others, like Russia, Mexico, and Japan, have yet to achieve high consumption economies, but could conceivably achieve them in the foreseeable future.

In the other part of the world, I will lump together all of Asia, except Japan and Israel, all of Africa, and most of the countries of Latin America. Here nations are very poor, and some may even be getting poorer. But more and more people in this part of the world are refusing to believe that their poverty is inevitable or divinely ordained. They are becoming increasingly aware of man's great power over nature and of the fact that they, as nations, anyway, can have at least some control over their own destiny. In most countries this awareness is still confined to a minority—sometimes even to a very small minority— but everywhere the leadership is aroused and wants to imitate the technology which made the other part of the world rich and powerful. These leaders want to bring about a renaissance and a reformation in their societies and to telescope into a few short decades all the social and economic change which came in the other part of the world only over a century or more. They are trying to usher their societies into an age of enlightenment.

This division of the world is made important largely through the spread of science and technology. It is said that science and technology have shrunk the world, and indeed they have. But they have also enlarged the world's problems out of all proportion with the past. Science and technology have forced the societies of the human race into an intimacy never before shared in history. At the same time, as Lord Russell has remarked, the first and foremost effect of the spread of science and technology has been to infuse humanity with an immense increase in the sense of human power—man's power over nature and over his fellow man. The combination of greater intimacy and

3

an immensely increased sense of human power has heightened the Babel of differences among the societies of mankind so that the degree of danger and discomfort in which we live together today is unique in modern history.

To the usual tasks of diplomacy these facts of modern life add a whole new dimension. To the age-old task of maintaining the balance of power must now be added the task of maintaining the balance of hope—hope in the proposition that the underdeveloped societies of the world can take science and technology into their lives without in the process denying the values of freedom and tolerance. It is to this problem that development diplomacy addresses itself.

Cooperation in economic development can be the most hopeful means, perhaps the only really important means, of maintaining this balance of hope. But the real advantages of such a cooperation must be separated from the false ones. The people of the rich countries must understand much better why they are called on to sacrifice some of their wealth to aid the poor countries. There must be a better understanding of what development has to do with tolerance and freedom, and of the kinds of change in conventional diplomatic practices that are called for. It is the task of those who practice development diplomacy to provide this understanding. It is a new and difficult task and in sketching some answers of my own I am fully aware of how fragmentary and inadequate they will be.

*   *

That vast stretch of the planet, extending eastward from Latin America, through Africa and the Middle East, to South and Southeast Asia, which we have come to call the underdeveloped world, is an area of great diversity. Here can be found virtually every race and creed which exists on earth, every kind of geographical environment and climate, and communities in widely differing stages of development. If most people are poor in the material things of life, there is in much of this area a wealth of resources waiting to be tapped. If the land in some places is dangerously overcrowded, in other places it could support two or three times the present population, even without much economic advance. These parts of the world would seem to defy useful generalizations.

However, by characterizing the nations of the underdeveloped world as entering upon an age of enlightenment I mean to suggest that they do have something in common. In fact, they have shared a common experience and are reacting to that experience in roughly similar ways. By choosing a phrase out of the literature of Western philosophy, I mean to suggest that the common experience they have shared is to have their traditional ways of life upset by the impact of the West's own Enlightenment as it found expression in the industrial revolution of the Western world.

Ever more widely over the past two hundred years, the philosophy and technology associated with the West's own Enlightenment have spread among societies whose customs and habits had hardly changed for centuries. In some places

5

change came with the first Western traders and investors who introduced plantation agriculture and an exchange economy where a subsistence economy had been the rule. In others it came with the mission schools where ideas of man's responsibility to better himself were taught and came into conflict with traditional obligations of the individual to his caste, tribe, or village community. It came with the mission doctor battling successfully against disease and robbing the witch doctor of his authority. It came with the first Western colonizers who interfered with the traditional structure of tribal or dynastic rule and started people on the road to thinking of themselves as nations in the Western sense.

The impact of these ideas and achievements was greatly reinforced with each scientific invention and each improvement in communications and transport. International wars played their part in exposing more and more millions to the paraphernalia of modern economic life. The cumulative result of all these invasions and intrusions has been to disturb the peace of tradition in almost every nook and cranny of the globe and touch off an historic transformation which today embraces the great majority of the world's people.

*　　*

This historic transformation is called, popularly, the revolution of rising expectations. But this can be a misleading slogan; not everybody is in revolt and the traditional "expectations" of people in these parts of the world are at least as strong as any expectations of a new life.

Perhaps the most dramatic rise in expectations has been the rise in life expectancy. Death rates in much of the underdeveloped world have fallen and fallen again. First, better transportation and the growth of commercial agriculture helped reduce the toll of famine. Then the spread of law and order reduced the toll of internal strife in many places. Latterly and spectacularly, the establishment of public health services in some underdeveloped countries has caused death rates in recent years to fall farther and faster than at any time or place in history.

The more dependents in a poor society—the more children to be fed, clothed, and educated—the less savings are available for investment in higher living standards. When this fact is combined with insufficient land to go around—as in Egypt and India, and on the island of Java, among other places today—rapid population growth can be a tragedy.

Not everywhere is population growth alarming; there is still plenty of land in most of Latin America, Africa, and even some Southeast Asian countries. And it is not that population is growing exceptionally fast; in most underdeveloped countries it is not growing abnormally fast in comparison with Western experience. The tragedy is that the population is beginning to rise at an earlier stage of economic and technological development than was true in Europe or North America. This greatly complicates the development problem. Science and technology, while sufficient to bring about a rapid and peaceful revolution in life expectancy at birth, have not proved sufficient to bring about a rapid and peaceful industrial revolution in order that there can be an expectancy of long life in even minimum comfort. In Ceylon, for example, where a special study of falling death rates has been undertaken, life expectancy at birth went up in the ten years between the years 1946 and 1957 as much as it rose in the United States in the fifty years between 1880 and 1930. This was brought about largely by the efficient application of a very cheap product—DDT. It cost the people of Ceylon only about $2.00 per head over the ten years to bring about this dramatic reduction in the death rate. The achievement hardly ruffled the surface of daily life. But in so far as there are more dependents to feed, clothe and educate, the lower death rate means higher development expenditures and greater urgency behind the changes needed for economic growth.

* *

One of the most important consequences of rising life expectancy in the underdeveloped world has been to deny millions their traditional expectation of a life on the land. In these countries the vast majority of the population still depends for its livelihood directly or indirectly on the land. But this is becoming increasingly difficult, and in many instances impossible.

In many countries traditional customs governing land

tenure have resulted in successive division and subdivision of land from generation to generation far beyond the limits of efficient farming. In India alone, already a population equal to the total population of Great Britain has been denied ownership of land and even tenancy; they have been forced, not into employment in the cities, but to live as chronically underemployed, landless farm laborers in conditions of extreme poverty and insecurity. And in addition to huge increases in the number of landless peasants, agricultural indebtedness has increased enormously until in many places there is little or no hope of ever discharging the burden of oppressive debt.

What we have here, then, is not rising expectations but the loss of traditional expectations. However inadequate the traditional ways of the rural population may be in the face of the onslaughts of technology, the hold of tradition on these people is a very strong one. And it is not wholly illogical by any means; the traditional societies of the world supplied many fundamental requirements for the human being which no amount of material progress has enabled him to live contentedly without. People living in these societies were accepted by their neighbors without question; they knew where they stood. They had a place in their communities, often an inherited trade. If they were not free as we know freedom, such was the security of their ancient ways that freedom had no meaning for them —unless it was something near to anarchy. If they are now attracted by the trappings and trinkets of modern economic life, we have no reason to think they desire to give up the security of their old ways for these things. In fact, so far as we know, most of those living in the rural areas of the underdeveloped world have not broadened their horizons much beyond their age-old desires for land enough to feed their families and freedom from oppressive debt.

The tragedy, of course, is that the impact of modern science and technology has made their traditional ways obsolete without as yet providing a tolerable alternative. Change is becoming the price of survival. This is clear to those millions who have crowded into the great urban centers, either attracted by the city lights or in the hope of earning enough to return to the land later. Here—whether it be Calcutta, Singapore, Cairo, Leopoldville, or the Port of Callao in Peru—the migrant finds how vast are the changes necessary to bring modern economic life to a traditional society.

The migrant to the city is perhaps the most cruelly treated by the historic transformation going on in the underdeveloped world. Away from the familiar ways of his native village, he is plunged into a bewildering, formless, insecure life, requiring a whole new set of attitudes towards life and work. If he is lucky enough to get a factory job, he is likely to find factory discipline irksome and pointless. If it is no great problem to teach him to operate a machine, often there is no common language with which to introduce him to such sophisticated ideas as quality control or the terms of a labor contract. Away from work he is more often than not herded into a wretched slum and exploited by the large, permanent underworld of beggars, vagrants, refugees, petty criminals, and the like who manage some-how to survive on the fringe economies of the cities of the underdeveloped world. The gulf between the securities of the old village ways and the rootless, seemingly aimless life of the city are often much too broad to be bridged even in a generation.

So it is wrong to say that the distinguishing feature of this so-called revolution of rising expectations is a universal desire to abandon old habits and attitudes towards life and work in favor of new ones. That might have been the case if the impact of Western ideas and philosophies had been as pervasive as the impact of Western science and technology. The apostles of a new life, as was the case in most modern revolutions, are the minority, typically those whose close contact with Western education, Western political thought, and Western material living standards has led them to want greater opportunities to practice their knowledge, greater outlets for their ambition, and a better material lot for their countrymen. Among these are the new leaders who make it possible for me to say that the underdeveloped world is entering on an age of enlightenment.

This class in the underdeveloped world constitutes a group privileged in relation to their countrymen, but a frustrated group nonetheless. The education and economic growth from which they are already benefiting have done much more to raise their aspirations and their desire for power than they have to provide them with opportunities for a productive life and outlets for their ambition. And there is no more explosive political material than the doctor who knows what modern medicine can do but does not have the facilities to put his knowledge to work; or the teacher who must teach, if at all, without textbooks; or the engineer without access to capital equipment; or the businessman without a place of business; or the politician without a following that understands what he is talking about.

This educated class is providing, quite logically, more and more of the architects and administrators of government in the underdeveloped world. In most former colonies they have already led their people to national independence. In all countries this aroused group now faces the infinitely more difficult task of carrying out a revolution within their own societies to prepare their people for modern economic life.

Few, if any, leaders in history faced a more ambitious task or one whose outcome was more uncertain. The governments in these countries are the primary agents of change in societies in which large numbers of people are resisting change. That governments play this role is not so much a matter of ideology as it is a matter of necessity. The politician and the bureaucrat in these countries are very literally leaders as well as rulers; they are taking the lead in trying to adapt to modern economic life ancient traditions which have been rendered tragically inadequate by the passage of time.

There is very little in the early development of Western countries which bears comparison with this task. In the age of inventions governments did not need to take many development initiatives; then the rate of growth was determined largely by the rate at which man could push ahead the frontiers of technology; then it made sense to allow the policies of government to be dictated to a large extent by the needs and initiatives of the private innovator. But now the knowledge about what it takes for a society to grow rich exists; the rate of growth, therefore, depends initially on how quickly society adapts itself to use this knowledge. In these circumstances it is hardly surprising that governments are performing many more innovating functions themselves and trying more deliberately to manipulate the lot of society. Such tendencies are spurred on by the fact that people are awakening more or less abruptly to the variety of achievements possible in modern economic society and are coming to want these achievements all at once. Leaders are driven to try to leap over the many contradictions in the economic development process, to try to settle once and for all the inevitable conflicts between growth and justice, growth and equality, growth and national power and prestige. No leaders in the early stage of the West's development faced anything like the range and complexity of choices which are faced by the new leaders of the underdeveloped world today.

And, of course, those who man the governments of the underdeveloped countries today are in a hurry; they are eager to imitate the technology which made Western nations rich and powerful. Often they have to hurry if they are to keep the inexorable pressure of population at bay. But they are also driven by a more fundamental urge;

they are driven by a renewed pride in their own racial and cultural heritage—a pride born partly of a genuine renaissance and partly of accumulated resentment over the gross inequalities in wealth among nations today and over real or imagined subjugation of their countries in the past. Nationalism is perhaps even more of a motive force among these new leaders than the drive to escape poverty. And often it is a nationalism that is only one part patriotism for every two parts an obsession that their poverty and discontent stem solely from having been held in tutelage by the strong.

It is difficult to exaggerate the importance of these new leaders. Their decisions will in large part determine not only the future course of their own countries, but increasingly the shape of international politics as well. And it is largely through these leaders that the old Western world, divided as it is into the camp of freedom and the camp of Communism, will exert whatever influence it will have on the revolution of rising expectations.

Communism has an insidious appeal to the new leaders of the underdeveloped world. On the one hand Communism blames all frustration, inequality, and poverty on Western exploitation. It plays heavily on the legacy of suspicion and animosity against the free West which the new leadership has inherited almost as an inevitable result of the transformation through which their countries are going. The world, according to the Communists, is riven by a sort of hideous class warfare between the have-not nations and the haves.

Then, again, Communism offers the appearance of a workable program to the frustrated elements among the educated—an outlet for personal ambition and a sense of participation in building national power. As evidence that this program works, the Communists point to Soviet Russia and Communist China, both underdeveloped countries only yesterday, which have pulled themselves up by their bootstraps until now they are great powers, feared by the West. Even the achievements of the Russians in outer space become part of the propaganda package designed to persuade all comers that the finest product of the Age of Enlightenment was Communism.

It would be disparaging the intelligence of the leaders of the underdeveloped countries to accuse any large number of them of taking very seriously this concoction of views about economics and history. Most are quite aware of the scars Communism has left on the Russian people and is leaving on the Chinese people; most hope desperately to avoid the inhumanity of Communist methods. At the same time they know that their people must make sacrifices to escape their poverty. Often their countries start from such a low point on the economic scale that the experience of the affluent West seems quite inappropriate to them. They sometimes feel that no model other than totalitarianism exists to give them hope of an early escape from the humiliations of poverty. If the free world has an alternative way to economic development that can approximate the rate of growth under Communism without the terrible cost to humanity which Communism entails, they do not yet see how that alternative applies to their particular situation.

*   *

Such is the background, it seems to me, of what is popularly called the revolution of rising expectations. It presents a challenge to Western civilization which bears comparison to any test faced by any of the great civilizations of history.

It is not so much a question of whether or not these countries develop; the pressures leave no alternative; only more economic development offers any hope of escape from the problems which economic development itself has already brought forth—escape from the problems of population pressure on the land and in the cities, escape from the problems of a lack of jobs and outlets for the ambitions of the educated. The question is, "How will development come?" The question is, "Can a poor society today escape its poverty without in the process generating extravagant forms of political injustice and cruelty?"

It is not so much the balance of political or economic power that is at stake here; rather, it is the balance of hope. If these countries cannot go through an age of enlightenment and reach a state where the accumulation of power in society is restrained by the checks and balances of free institutions, then in all likelihood the balance of hope will be tipped towards a future which is incompatible with liberty—not just in these parts of the world, but everywhere.

This challenge would test the mettle of Western civilization even if Communism were not the force which it is in world politics today. Communism did not cause the historic transformation going on in the underdeveloped world; the ideas and achievements of Communism do not give to that transformation its historic importance. It is the ideas and achievements that came out of the West's own Englightenment which were the primary cause. All that Communism does is to make more obvious the challenge of the underdeveloped world and more urgent the events that occur there.

And what an ironic situation it is! Communism in the underdeveloped world poses as the modern champion of the ideas of the Age of Enlightenment—the champion of scientific thought and of technology, of nationalism and democracy; those nations from which came virtually all the real revolutionaries of the past two hundred years are cast in the role of reactionaries. At the same time, in the underdeveloped world the first and most fundamental result of the impact of these ideas and achievements has been to make it increasingly impossible for individual freedom and tolerance among nations to coexist for long alongside mass poverty. Clearly, if the Western nations cannot persevere now with their works and their ideals in these parts of the world, today's irony will be tomorrow's tragedy.

Obviously no conventional calculation of economic advantage or political strategy can produce a suitable response to this predicament. The West's security is threatened not so much by any clear and present political, economic, or military danger in these parts of the world as it is by a possible loss of its own political and economic dynamic. What is needed from the West is what might be called a new sense of vocation in the world—that is, a willingness to work, adventurously, at concrete tasks simply as a means of seeking constructive contacts with other nations and other peoples in the belief that in this way the balance of hope in a future consistent with the spread of individual freedom and tolerance among nations will be maintained. Without capturing such a sense of vocation, it is, I think, quite inadequate to talk of the economic benefits which might accrue to the West through trading with and investing in a more prosperous and productive world; these benefits will not materialize unless Western nations allow their acts to express more than just a desire for economic advantage. Nor is it enough to talk about an integration of political aims and ideals between the West and these parts of the world; there will be no such integration unless it grows out of a long period of constructive contact in tasks of common interest.

When I speak of a "sense of vocation" I am not referring to a ringing declaration of a bold new program. What is required is a new awareness of the predicament of free peoples in this age out of which can come a new sense of purpose. We can, if we want, find as many adventurous avenues open to us as our "enlightened" ancestors did. We can develop a new sense of vocation in these parts of the world quite worthy of the best in Western traditions. For there is glaring us in the face the antagonist that calls us to this vocation; it exists in the very poverty which Western civilization has done so much to make intolerable.

The West's response to the historic transformation going on in the underdeveloped world should be, I think, to undertake a series of adventures designed to engineer an escape from the worst pangs of poverty. It should do this for its own sake in order to provide a means of reasserting its own identity with the ideals of liberty and tolerance.

It is not that there is any certain and established relationship between economic progress and the values of freedom and tolerance. There is no such relationship; economic development is a fickle process; it destroys old habits and attitudes toward life even as it creates the wherewithal for a better material life; it creates human desires often much faster than it provides the means for their gratification; its one continual and overriding requirement is change; by itself it leads nowhere in particular and may lead anywhere in general.

But part of facing the realities of this world is recognizing that economic development, while not sufficient, is necessary for progress towards all of the political, economic, and humanitarian aims which the free peoples believe in and seek beyond their shores. By choosing to make it their special purpose to help find ways out of poverty the free nations are serving the ideal of freedom in the most tangible way open to them.

Professor Tillich once invented the phrase "belief-ful realism" and it expresses well what I have in mind. If the West is to exert a continuing and constructive influence on the historic transformation going on in the under-developed world, it must make a multiplicity of contacts with its leaders and its people; it must seek working partnerships capable of functioning in spite of the passions which bedevil normal diplomatic and economic relations. Such a course is the realistic course; for only with time and through working side by side at tasks of mutual concern can the West make good the promise of economic benefits, tolerant political relations, and human betterment. And economic development provides the best tasks, perhaps the only really important ones, through which such contacts can be made and maintained.

At the same time there is no better way in which the West can signal its belief in a future compatible with liberty. By concentrating on the infinite possibilities which lie hidden in this historic transformation, the West can cultivate a new sense of adventure. Like all adventures, this will require the courage to live with doubt about the outcome and a willingness to make sacrifices. But how else save through accepting doubt and sacrifice can we test the real worth of the knowledge which came to "enlightened" man?

II ←←←←←←←←←←←←←←←←←←←←←←←←←←←←←←←←←←←←←

The Diplomacy
of Economic Aid

I HAVE characterized what is going on in
the underdeveloped world as an historic transformation. It
would seem unnecessary then, to point out that it is likely
to be with us for a very long while. Yet it *is* necessary to
underline this point since so much of the discussion of
economic aid today concerns a search for some simple,
short-term way of turning that transformation into freedom and viability within a brief span of years.

I am afraid that much of the reason for this misdirected
search stems from the blinding success of the Marshall
Plan. Without detracting from that unique achievement,
I am compelled to say that it bears almost no comparison
to the present problem; in fact, it is useful only as a
contrast.

The governments participating in the Marshall Plan
shared a common heritage and a common and clearly defined predicament. The political and economic aims of one
nation found, if not a ready response, at least a sympathetic
hearing in the others. A clear, limited, and concrete objective presented itself—that of restoring the economic

strength and financial independence lost in war. It was possible to measure usefully, if not entirely precisely, the economic resources needed to achieve that objective. And there was in prospect a handy measurement, the re-establishment of substantial currency convertibility to judge when the necessary production and per capita income levels had been reached.

None of these conditions exists in the problem we are now considering. Between the rich nations and the poor nations there is little common heritage, and, in so far as there is a common predicament, it suggests no simple, short-term escape. The immediate political and economic aims of one nation in the group often complete or collide head-on with the immediate political and economic aims of the others. To the extent that there is an agreed objective for economic aid, it is to help the leaders of the poor nations to lead their countrymen out of the worst of poverty. Since this objective is neither limited nor concrete, there can be no really useful measure of the economic resources needed to achieve it. And while reasonable financial equilibrium is a necessary concomitant of orderly growth, the balance of payments is not a useful measure of how much per capita income and production will permit a tolerable order in the underdeveloped world.

The policy problem is altogether different and so are most of the operational problems. It is one thing to aid the recovery of industry, for example, in a country where there has been considerable experience with the technical and managerial problems involved. It is something else again to help launch new industries in countries that must initially import the necessary technical and managerial skills and in communities where there has not been any experience with factory life. It is no small problem just to find trained people in the world willing to undertake tasks like this, to say nothing of the many problems involved in trying to get agreement from an underdeveloped country to accept the authority of foreign technicians and managers in their special fields.

I list these contrasts—and there are more—not to belittle what was done under the Marshall Plan; it stands as one of the boldest and most imaginative diplomatic achievements in history. I list them only to show that we have before us now a brand new diplomatic problem of vastly greater dimensions.

The plain fact is that the conditions for a full integration of the political and economic aims of the rich and the poor nations in the free world community do not exist, nor is it possible to foresee a time in the future when they will. For the rich nations the problem is to live constructively with the historic transformation going on in the under-developed world, not to try to "solve" it.

The values of freedom and democracy cannot be sold like soap; nor are they the necessary result of economic development. People in the West came to respect these values only gradually over many years. If respect for them is to spread among the people of the underdeveloped world, the West must be willing to work side by side with these people and make common cause with them. For it is not by any sudden act of conversion, but only through growing together over time that the West can hope its values will take root and spread. This growing together will take constant and constructive contact and that is what the exercise of economic aid—or development diplomacy as I have called it—is all about.

*   *

Development diplomacy is such a new art in the affairs of nations that before it can earn for itself a recognizable status in the policies of the Western nations there must be a greater understanding of its specific aims and objectives. And since I will argue that economic aid cannot be effective without a separate and distinct status in the policies of these nations, let us first consider at some length just what these aims and objectives are.

The development diplomat must fill the gap between the conventional diplomat and the trader and the investor. His aim should not be commercial or strictly economic; but neither should he be concerned with the narrow political objectives which sometimes overburden the regular diplomat. The development diplomat should be a man with a vocation, rather than a man with immediate terms of reference. As an artisan of economic development he should use the tools of economics and other disciplines as best he can to place in perspective, to shed light on and to illuminate the choices before the decision-makers in the underdeveloped world.

When I say, "illuminating the choices," I refer to the

problem which economists call "the allocation of resources." Now it is not economists but politicians, civil
servants, and businessmen who decide, for the most part,
how the resources of a country are allocated. The professional job of the economist is, or should be, to make the
politician, civil servant, and businessman aware of the
economic consequences of their decisions, and to provide
evidence on which the decision-makers can weigh the benefits and costs of alternative courses of action. The hope
the economist holds out is that there will be a "better"
allocation of resources if decisions are taken with the
knowledge of their economic consequences. This is the
same hope development diplomacy holds out.

This may sound like a strange role for a diplomat, but
as a practical matter in the modern world it promises to be
the most effective way in which the free nations can exercise a constructive influence on the development of the
underdeveloped countries. The task of illuminating choices
goes right to the root of the development problem, which
is often said to be a lack of resources, or of savings, or of
education, or of entrepreneurship. These are all part of
the problem, but it is more useful, I think, to look at it in
terms of the decisions needed to make more of the potential
for growth that already exists—decisions to organize idle
time for productive work; decisions to transform unpro-
ductive investment; decisions to turn a classical, Western
course of study into a course of study more relevant to an
underdeveloped country, and so on. Each of these decisions
involves making choices. Usually the choices must be made

on the basis of very imprecise and fragmentary evidence. But it can be said that in so far as these choices are made without regard to the economic consequences, they are much less likely to yield "good" decisions in terms of growth, tolerance, freedom, and all the other aims which free nations believe in and seek beyond their shores. Thus, we can say that by illuminating the choices before the decision-makers—whether they be politicians, businessmen or bureaucrats—development diplomacy performs a very practical task and one no other kind of diplomacy is directly concerned with.

But to put some meat on the bones of these ideas let us examine this notion of development diplomacy in action.

* *

Very often people come into my office after having visited some country or other in the underdeveloped world to tell me what they think is wrong with that country. And I am told that the trouble with country X is that the people won't work; the trouble with country Y is that there is a desperate need for outside capital; and the trouble with country Z is a lack of entrepreneurs. In each case it is some obstacle, more or less immovable, that is seen to be standing in the way of progress.

The pessimists among these visitors point to the social and political obstacles in the way of growth—whether they be India's sacred cows or the nationalistic oil policy of Brazil—and conclude that the World Bank is definitely wasting its money making loans to these countries. The optimists, on the other hand, urge the Bank to redouble its lending because they believe that all that is needed to redeem the situation is more money.

Piecing these fragmentary observations together, one gets the picture of a field strewn with obstacles, some of which are immovable and others of which can be pushed aside. So far as it goes, this is not an inaccurate picture, but it is not complete; it lacks a dynamic element. It reality the obstacles in the path of development are changing form and character all the time because in reality economic development and social change are interacting all the time. In the underdeveloped world today society is continually adapting itself to make use of existing knowledge. Development is proceeding *in spite of* the cultural attitudes, social institutions, and political conflicts which sometimes seem to be such immovable barriers. It is not a smooth, uninterrupted progression, to be sure; rather, growth appears more as a series of fits and starts. "And yet," as Galileo is supposed to have said, "it moves!"

It is really not just a lack of capital per se, of savings per se, of education per se, of entrepreneurship per se, and so forth, which stands in the way of more rapid growth in the underdeveloped world. It is more useful, I think, to consider the problem in terms of how to achieve the kinds of decisions which are needed to make more of the potential for growth. For as there is a greater awareness of the possibilities for growth in society, many of the traditional obstacles appear much less formidable.

Take entrepreneurship, for example, which is often cited

as the key development component that is missing. We do not really know where entrepreneurs come from. If in England, entrepreneurs appeared among nonconformist traders, in Japan they sprang from the ranks of the petty nobility—the samurai. In India, the growth of entrepreneurship has been very complex, involving as it has the cultural background of sect and caste and the unique institution of the managing agency. There is room for a lot of speculation about where entrepreneurs come from; but it *is* speculation. All we know for certain is that once people become conscious of the possibility of economic development in their society, entrepreneurs start appearing. There has been a veritable flowering of entrepreneurs in Latin America over the past thirty years and in Pakistan and Turkey in the short period since World War II. We can confidently expect further such outbreaks as development takes hold in the underdeveloped world.

What is true of entrepreneurship is broadly true of all the requisites for economic growth. As more people become conscious of the possibility of a better material life through a different use of their time, energy, and savings, there will be more productive work and more productive savings. By illuminating the choices before the decision-makers, development diplomacy promotes such a consciousness and in this way helps to remove obstacles in the path of development.

This does not mean that direct attacks on some of these obstacles—the direct provision of development capital or the encouragement of new forms of education—are unimportant; on the contrary, they are indispensable instruments of development diplomacy. But as has been said time and time again and cannot be repeated too often, no nation can supply another nation with more than a tiny fraction of the resources needed for self-sustaining growth; the road to self-sustaining growth must be built by the poor society itself. Therefore, the most important task development diplomacy can perform is to illuminate the choices that must be made in the building of that road.

Initially, illuminating choices involves asking questions. This is easiest to illustrate in terms of specific projects. The mere fact that a river runs downhill very fast, to take a simple example, is not sufficient reason to build a power dam. First a whole lot of questions have to be asked—and some kind of answers fashioned.

One must ask whether the construction of a power dam would meet some important objective; that is, would it provide power for a market that already exists or is in prospect? Would it provide irrigation waters for land which can be made arable in this way and on which farmers might be willing to settle? Would it provide benefits in terms of flood control? Then one must ask whether a big power dam is the best way of meeting any or all of these objectives. Alternative possibilities, such as a thermal power plant or a simple irrigation barrage, or both, have to be considered as possible choices.

And there are financial questions which have to be asked. In the Bank we deal mostly with large and expensive public utilities—port facilities, power projects, railroads, and the like. Obviously, if there is to be a rational allocation of resources in terms of growth, politicians, civil servants, and utility managers must have a good idea of the real costs of these investment proposals. And since these projects can gobble up huge amounts of capital, rational decisions on whether and how to invest in them have vital importance for economic growth.

Before deciding what the real cost of capital is, it is, of course, necessary to make the best use possible of the data available. Adequate technical preparation of a project is such an obvious necessity that it hardly needs elaboration, but development diplomacy will fail if it overlooks the obvious. And often adequate preparation of a project is more a matter of good organization than of modern technology—more a matter of simply keeping separate and complete accounts than of adopting elaborate new accounting methods.

Sometimes the weight of evidence points to fairly definite answers to the questions development diplomacy must ask in project analysis; sometimes there is a clear saving in efficiency in one alternative over the other. At other times there are no very precise answers. For example, we once had a spirited argument in the Bank over whether a mining company that approached us for a loan to buy modern mining machinery would do more to increase productivity if instead it borrowed locally to build new houses for the miners. Obviously this is a question the answer to which is not subject to very precise calculation. But it is worth while asking the question nonetheless. Illuminating choices in project analysis is not just a matter of minimizing waste, though that is very important. And it is not that there is very often one, absolutely right answer. The important thing is to encourage the habit of weighing benefits and costs. When that habit becomes ingrained, society is already most of the way to becoming development-minded.

Specific development projects provide the handiest illustration of what "the illumination of choices" means. But this is just the beginning of the story. Economic development cannot be described simply in terms of a series of projects, designed in a technological vacuum and unrelated to broader economic and political issues. Economic development involves, in addition to projects, the preparation of an economic plan and the relation at the highest level of plan and projects to the formulation of a national policy of which economic policy is only one part. Unless these three sides of economic development—projects, planning, and policy—are seen, not as three separate compartments of a box, but as three aspects of a single problem the shape of which is changing all the time, nobody concerned with economic development—neither the politician, nor the businessman, nor the development diplomat—will be in a position to judge usefully the economic consequences of a given decision or of alternative decisions.

It is in the planning process that development diplomacy finds its greatest challenge. The planning process should be the place where there are the greatest opportunities for illuminating choices and where the development diplomat should make his most important contribution. But unfortunately planning is still a very new concept and there is no broad consensus about the aims and objectives of the exercise. In fact, there are few more controversial words in the lexicon of development diplomacy. The concept of planning is bedeviled equally by the suffocating embraces of its idealistic champions and the cynical shafts of its detractors.

Between the idealists, who are more interested in imposing solutions than in illuminating choices, and the cynics who distrust planning in all its interpretations, lies, I think, a rational definition of the concept which should be nourished. Planning, simply defined, should be the place where the political leader is faced with an awareness of the consequences of his decisions before he makes them instead of afterwards. Taking the definition one step further, it should be the means by which the lines of communication are kept open between those who make decisions, those who "illuminate" them, and those who carry them out.

Whatever outward form planning takes, if it does not keep these lines of communication open, there will be a mess. For example, in one country I know of a development plan was prepared simply on somebody's assumption of the rate of growth that was desirable, "needed," or otherwise divined from national income analyses. Further assumptions were made of the capital that would be needed in various sectors of the economy to produce the output that was assumed to be needed. A massive document was drawn up on these abstract assumptions, with no attempt made to find out whether the necessary finance might be forthcoming or whether the plan conformed to the realities of the many, often quite legitimate, political claims on the country's resources. When all the work was completed, the head of the local planning commission admitted that it was really just an academic exercise and could not be taken seriously.

In this case it was just time and talent wasted. But I suspect in other cases plans drawn up this way become tantamount to the law of the land and have been the cause of more than one unnecessary financial crisis. This can be dangerous.

I am not criticizing the tools of economics, but the misuse of them. Unless planning involves first and foremost a bringing together of the existing claims on a country's resources—that is, unless it is based not on a single assumption, but on an appropriate range of assumptions, some induced and some deduced—the tools of economics cannot be safely and efficiently employed as a means of illuminating choices. Neither economics nor any other academic discipline in and of itself tells us just what the shape and the magnitude of investment ought to be in a given country. These disciplines can suggest orders of magnitude and help us to judge whether plans, projects, and policy are well related to one another. But they cannot make economic development any less of a three-sided problem. Plans and projects must be checked and co-ordinated with the actual possibilities, with what people really want in the way of growth and change and with what they are prepared to sacrifice. Otherwise, planning can lead at best to waste and at worst to the encouragement of extravagant forms of coercion.

There is a fundamental principle here as well as a matter of efficiency. At any given time, in any country, rich or poor, there is a conflict between the demands of growth itself and the demands which growth is supposed to serve. At any given time there is a conflict between the demands of growth and the demands for social welfare; between the demands of growth and the demands for economic security and employment for all; between the demands of growth and the demands of national power and prestige; between the demands of growth and the demands for cultural development. In the poor countries today these conflicts are particularly acute. Leaders there, as have leaders in all developing countries in modern times, want growth so that their countries can be strong and powerful; so that their people can have more jobs, modern social services and a more equitable distribution of income; so that they can assert their cultural renaissance with visible symbols of national prestige. But always at any give time there must be a choice between more of these ends and more of growth itself. And against the background of mass poverty the choice is always agonizing.

Today the political leaders of the poor countries, besides having to reconcile traditional attitudes toward life and work, also have to reconcile most of the competing and conflicting objectives found in richer societies. Reconciling these objectives is a political, not an economic, problem. The economics of growth simply says that every time the demands of growth are overridden there is a price: the poor will remain poorer for longer. Whether planning transforms the tools of economics into useful political, as well as useful economic, tools or simply turns them into bludgeons with which to coerce society, depends fundamentally on whether planning is used as a means of illuminating choices or as a means of imposing solutions.

The use of planning largely to keep the lines of communication open among those who make decisions, those who "illuminate" them, and those who carry them out, is the most effective way to achieve a rational and democratic resolution of the conflicts and contradictions which are inherent in the growth process. If only it encourages the asking of the right questions, planning cannot help but promote better answers in terms of growth. Furthermore, it can encourage policy-makers to focus upon the necessity for engineering an escape from poverty and to make this idea a catalyst for transforming into constructive patriotism the nationalism which is rampant in the underdeveloped world.

For development diplomacy all this has rather obvious and immediate implications. Development diplomacy must recognize that if planning is regarded as a means of illuminating choices rather than of imposing solutions, then planning everywhere always involves a series of political struggles. And the development diplomat cannot be effective if he ignores this fact or tries to remain above the struggle. While he is the partisan of growth, he cannot claim any absolute authority for his criteria; he knows that no matter how poor a country may be, there will be many occasions when considerations of justice or defense will necessarily override them. And because he is in a political struggle, he knows there will be other occasions on which he will be overridden by considerations much less compelling. This means he always has to work out the economics of the second, third, or fourth "best" allocation of resources in terms of economic growth. But this does not mean that he is thereby rendered ineffective. If development diplomacy to be successful required imposing some grand design on an underdeveloped country, then the game would not be worth the candle even if it were possible to play it in this way. The strength of development diplomacy lies precisely in not becoming part of some grand design, but in illuminating choices in the real world where economic development and social change are interacting all the time.

In talking about planning, I would not want to give the impression that all decisions have to be made at some central point. Indeed, nothing can be so deadening as a process in which every "t" has to be crossed by the highest authority. Apart from anything else, it denies opportunity for local or individual initiative. Initiative is priceless. To hold it within the general lines of national policy is one thing; to treat it as though it were of purely secondary consequence is another. Initiative should be encouraged wherever it is found, whether it be the personal initiative of the entrepreneur, the group initiative of a co-operative, or the local political initiative of a town or a province.

How to achieve a consistent policy line while still leaving room for private and local initiative is one of the most difficult arts of planning. Here is no place for dogma; it is folly in the face of the wide variety of economic experience in the world to suppose that what works in one country at one stage of development necessarily will work in another country at a different stage. At the same time the kinds of choices which politicians, bureaucrats, and businessmen face in this matter can often be illuminated quite simply and dispassionately. For example, where there are private entrepreneurs willing and able to do development jobs, it is not necessary to appeal to ideology to make clear the loss which the community will suffer if they are denied their place in national plans. It is not necessary to appeal to ideology to make clear to the civil servant that both he and the private entrepreneur will have more time and energy for their respective tasks if general guidance of the private sector can be substituted for direct controls. Nor is it necessary to appeal to ideology to make clear the advantages of a development initiative by state or local government if the alternative is no initiative at all.

Again the strength of the development diplomat lies in illuminating choices, not in trying to impose solutions. If he is to succeed, he must be a man with a vocation, not a man with an ideological mission. And in no place is this more important than in the planning process, beset as it inevitably is with the most vexing of conflicts. I believe that out of today's planning procedures in many underdeveloped countries can grow a habit of resolving conflicts in a

37

rational and democratic manner which may prove eventually the most important means of encouraging a public respect for free institutions. And development diplomacy, much more than any other kind of diplomacy, will have an important part in determining whether or not this comes to pass.

But development diplomacy needs the backing of substantial capital; unlike some other branches of the art, it is not possible to succeed in this kind of diplomacy by just talking a good game. Development diplomacy needs capital because it must be a working diplomacy, capable of pointing to visible results at any given time. Development diplomacy needs capital because it needs to point to concrete development projects, the tangible proof that it is helping to engineer an escape from poverty.

And development diplomacy needs contacts; lines of communication of its own everywhere in the underdeveloped world; contacts with men and women to whom the right kinds of development decisions are an integral part of their own professional outlook; contacts with men and women who speak the language of economics without the taint of ideology. Right now there exists a very sizable guild of these men and women in the underdeveloped world; I know, because if there were not, the World Bank would not have been able over the last fourteen years to participate in some six hundred different development projects in fifty different countries. But these people need help and encouragement; development diplomacy must build on its contacts and continually make new ones.

Finally, development diplomacy must have a status in the national policies of the Western nations—not an overriding status, but a separate and distinct status which will allow it to function in spite of the bitter controversies of our times. Just as the development diplomat is a man with a vocation, so development diplomacy, if it is to succeed, must reflect a new sense of vocation in the West towards the historic transformation going on in the underdeveloped world. This is the problem to which I will return since the kind of adventure I have in mind must start right here in the West.

III ‹‹‹‹‹‹‹‹‹‹‹‹‹‹‹‹‹‹‹‹‹‹‹‹‹‹‹‹‹‹‹‹‹‹‹‹‹‹‹

A Status for Development

In the year 1580 the English historian and geographer, Richard Hakluyt, wrote a set of instructions to the gentlemen merchants of the "Moscovie Company" in which he said:

"If you find any island or maine land populous, and that same people hath neede of cloth, then you are to advise what commodities they have to purchase the same withal. If they be poore, then you are to consider the soile and how by any possibilities the same may be made to enrich them, that hereafter they may have something to purchase the cloth withal."

Here we have technical assistance as a means of promoting export markets in the year 1580!

But in those days, as in these, concern for development in international affairs was much more than just a business concern. Under the mercantilist system it was one way to colonies and foreign trade monopolies through which the monarchs of the time enhanced their power and wealth at home and abroad. It was not a benign diplomacy; mercantilist practices were the root cause of many wars, indeed a significant cause of the American revolution.

During the century or so when laissez-faire trade flourished, it was thought that the same ends were best reached through relying on market forces. Thus Adam Smith was able to write, "Little else is requisite to carry a state to the highest degree of opulence from the lowest barbarism but peace, easy taxes and a tolerable administration of justice; all the rest being brought about by the natural course of things." By "the natural course of things" Smith meant market forces. To Britain, which pioneered the industrial revolution, this doctrine for a time made sense in terms of its national interest, and, while it did, development was strictly a private venture.

But gradually the ideology of laissez-faire became honored more in the breach than in practice. Even as early as 1850 the British Government was again taking a big hand in overseas development. Parliament stepped in to acquire land for new railways in India and to guarantee investors a 5 per cent return on any capital they invested in the enterprise. British consuls around the world were allowed once more to trade on their own account, as they were accustomed to in mercantilist days. And the British Government —and Navy—became unhesitant in responding to appeals for protection from private investors and trading companies.

Looking back on the laissez-faire period from the vantage point of the 1920's, the economic historian, Leland Jenks, was frankly "astonished" that it lasted as long as it did. In the 1840's, in Latin America alone, Jenks pointed out, "Fifty million pounds in foreign government bonds were in default with unpaid dividends from five to twenty years overdue. Yet the Foreign Office did not land the marines or take over the Treasury of a single country." But by the middle of the century conditions began to change; and of Europe and America at the turn of the century Jenks wrote, "It is customary for modern States, like the United States under (Theodore) Roosevelt or Great Britain under Salisbury or Grey to do something on behalf of bondholders—something dramatic and not necessarily inexpensive; customs control, . . . armed intervention, political sterilization"—diplomacy then provided a bag of tricks to astonish the unwary issuer of bonds. It all sounds so very old-fashioned, but that was what "development diplomacy" was like in the seventy years before World War I.

And it had its bizarre moments. Consider the spectacle of Republican France helping Czarist Russia to sell to the good citizens of France the equivalent, at today's prices, of $2.5 billion worth of 5 and 6 per cent bonds, at a time when the Russian Government was spending half its borrowings on arms and armaments and meeting an increasingly large percentage of its ordinary expenses from the proceeds of the sale of alcohol. A French colleague of mine remembers all too well the day his father papered the wall of a room in his house in Southern France with defaulted Russian bonds; his father had sold a sizable piece of real estate to buy those bonds; that piece of real estate is now a very fashionable Riviera resort!

With the Great Depression, trading nations turned in

upon themselves and development again became a matter of promoting exports and of searching for raw materials. It was to promote American exports that the Export-Import Bank was established in 1935 and the idea of reciprocal trade agreements enacted into legislation the year before. But before the Depression was really over, World War II was on and development diplomacy became a very minor consideration. Even at Bretton Woods in 1944, where the World Bank and the International Monetary Fund were born, the idea of development aid for the poor countries of the world was more or less an afterthought. It was the Fund, not the Bank, that occupied the attention of the delegates. The major concern was the reconstruction of Europe and of an international trading system designed to meet the needs of the European and Atlantic countries. The World Bank was called officially the International Bank for Reconstruction *and Development*, but it was reconstruction that was the dominant concern immediately after Bretton Woods.

In the event, the Bank's reconstruction phase was short-lived. It rapidly became apparent that the task was far beyond the Bank's resources and not capable of being handled on a "bankable" basis. It took the Marshall Plan to accomplish the reconstruction task, and while the Marshall Plan was dominant the needs of the underdeveloped countries remained subordinate in the policies of the Western nations. While President Roosevelt had included "freedom from want" in his famous "Four Freedoms" speech during World War II and President Truman had added his Point

43

Four program in 1950, it is only in the past few years that Western nations have regarded the development of under-developed countries as an objective of first importance. It is only now that Western nations are beginning to give development diplomacy a separate and distinct status in their policies.

To accord the conscious and deliberate promotion of economic growth in foreign lands such importance in policy and to implement this aim on the scale on which, in fact, it has been implemented in the past few years finds no precedent in history. It is not surprising, then, that public officials are in the habit of citing a variety of motives for their actions in this area, and that conventional economic and diplomatic arguments are often stretched to cover rather awkwardly the novel situations created by the need to justify large economic aid programs. If it really is just narrow economic or political advantage which the West is after with economic aid, then it is hard to explain why there should be a need to expand and intensify this effort.

What is happening, I think, is that the development of these lands is gradually coming to be accepted as something of an end in itself because development diplomacy is proving a more practical way of dealing with events in the underdeveloped world than is conventional diplomacy. Let us examine some of the stated national interests of the Western nations to see how far this is so, for it is my contention that development diplomacy, to be successful, requires the acceptance of development aid as a more or less permanent

44

feature of Western policy with a separate and distinct status of its own.

*   *

Economic aid, particularly in the United States, is still talked of primarily as a tactical weapon in the Cold War. This is hardly surprising. I have already said that the existence of Communism as a world force lends urgency to events in the new nations of the underdeveloped world—some new in fact, others new in spirit. And I have said that Communism makes clear and present the dangers inherent in the historic transformation that is going on so largely as the result of the impact of Western civilization. Certainly Communism provides a motivation which can hardly be ignored.

But the idea of a "tactical weapon" implies the existence of a strategy and I often wonder just where economic aid fits into that strategy. The relationship between economic aid and the security of the Western nations is indeed a direct one; I have suggested that economic aid should be the principal means by which the West maintains its political and economic dynamic in the underdeveloped world. This is quite consistent with the West's desire to prevent the spread of Communism, and in the long run this may be the most effective way of encouraging the growth of durable free institutions in the developing countries. But economic aid cannot serve such a function if it is simply regarded as a tactic in some kind of competitive exercise with Communism.

The so-called competition between Communism and the West is, I am afraid, being conducted too often these days on the Communists' terms, and this, more than any other single factor, is preventing the full exploitation of the possibilities of development diplomacy. To try to compete with the Communists on their own terms is to reduce the "illumination of choices," which I have described as the essential business of development diplomacy, to little more than an auction between the great powers in the Cold War. I suggest that this is a bad bargain for the West.

The issue is this: Are the political interests of the West better served by administering economic aid in an effort to outbid the Russians for public favor in the underdeveloped world? Or are they better served by administering aid with the single-minded purpose of providing something which the underdeveloped countries require for more rapid growth? If the West is to use aid primarily to court the favor of the underdeveloped countries and to woo them away from the Communists, it should be recognized that aid can all too easily play into the Communists' hands. It can all too easily result in channeling resources into uneconomic projects and programs, thereby subverting the economies of the underdeveloped countries rather than strengthening them. Surely, the choice should be to contribute something that is really required for economic growth. This may mean that in the propaganda battle the West will often have to settle for letting virtue be its own reward; however, such a settlement is, I suggest, quite in keeping with the real security interests of the West.

Nor does it make sense in terms of the security interests of the West to let it appear that competition with Communism means that the West, like the Communists, wants to use aid to impose some particular kind of economic or political system on the underdeveloped countries. The West should stress the *diversity* of its political and economic institutions for it is this diversity which, more than anything, sets Western ways apart from Communist ways. Out of a great variety of views about the role of economic activity in society, many different nations in the Western world grew rich, without sacrificing their liberties. This is the example the West should hold forth.

* *

There have been some occasions, not necessarily connected directly with the Cold War, when I have been tempted to believe that development diplomacy has no status at all in the strategy of the Western powers. Economic aid has been used all too frequently in recent years in an effort to bring about some temporary accommodation in conventional diplomacy—as a reward for a military alliance or a diplomatic concession, or as a last-ditch attempt to retrieve a diplomatic miscalculation. On such occasions the recipient nation has concluded, as well it might, that its part of the bargain is fulfilled when the treaty is signed or the vote in the United Nations taken. The development aspects of the bargain have been little more than window dressing.

I will not attempt to judge whether the price of using

47

aid in this way has been worth it or not. It is enough to say that from the point of view of development the price has been very high, especially where aid bestowed for some narrow political end has abetted and perpetuated policies which make growth impossible. This cost must be figured into the cost of any temporary accommodation which the diplomatists and military strategists may have secured.

In contrast, if economic aid is accorded a separate and distinct status in national policy, development diplomacy can help conventional diplomacy. In so far as it brings about a more durable contact between the Western nations and the underdeveloped nations—the kind of contact which may remain open when conventional diplomacy breaks down—then it offers the hope that there may be less need for expensive and often self-defeating temporary accommodations.

The World Bank and the other development agencies of the United Nations already have had some experience to bear out this point. Two cases attracting considerable publicity are the negotiations with the United Arab Republic regarding the claims and counterclaims which followed after the Suez crisis, and the continuing negotiations between India and Pakistan over the division of the waters of the Indus Basin. In both of these cases conventional diplomacy failed; in the one case a war was fought and in the other there has been an ever-present threat of war. In the case of the United Arab Rebublic, the Bank was able to act as a successful channel for negotiations, not because of any feats of personal diplomacy, not because the basic causes of tension were removed, but because the Bank was in working contact with all parties and able to use that position to resolve arguments. While a development institution alone cannot solve fundamental disputes between nations, it can often turn the edge of such disputes by directing the attention and efforts of the nations toward absorption in their own development.

The Indus negotiations are still in progress, but I have hope that they, too, will result in agreement. If Pakistan and India can escape their predicament in this crucial matter of dividing the waters in the largest irrigation system in the world by turning their joint efforts to the development of that system, then the whole world will benefit. Certainly the six nations which have pledged capital to support an agreed program of development will have provided a signal example of the possibilities of development diplomacy.

These were spectacular examples and perhaps there will be more comparable to them. But the real work of development diplomacy hardly ever makes the front pages. It is the hard work of helping to plan, execute, and follow up on a host of development programs and projects in the underdeveloped world, some of which may take a decade or more to come into full use. It is the business of coming to know those who make the decisions and talk the language of development dispassionately and of establishing a working partnership with them. It is the business of forging new ties among nations to replace old ties that have been broken more or less abruptly in recent times.

And there is still a great deal of unexplored territory in development diplomacy. Over the long run it is, I am confident, through exploring this territory that the Western nations can best serve their political interests in the underdeveloped world. It is by giving development diplomacy a separate and distinct status in national policy—a status apart from the tactical problems posed by the existence of Communism as a world force and apart from other narrow political and military interests—that the West can best influence the course of events in the underdeveloped world in directions compatible with liberty and tolerance. I do not say that development diplomacy should ignore the problems which concern conventional diplomacy; I do say that it should hold out the hope of continued constructive contact in spite of them.

*   *

What is true of the political interest of the old nations of the free world is also true of the economic interest of these nations. Expanding trade and investment between these parts of the world depends now on a quite fundamental break with past attitudes and practices. Where a trader's outlook sufficed in the past, an investor's outlook is needed now. And again this boils down to recognizing the status of development diplomacy.

This is particularly true for trade. The simple idea of "growth through trade" no longer satisfies the underdeveloped world today as it did, by and large, even a generation ago. This is not true for all countries; but it is true for those countries that are trying to push their development along under forced draft. And as more countries undertake to do this, the problem of maintaining conditions for a healthy and expanding trade is likely to be even more difficult than it is now.

Why is it going to be more difficult? It is because all too often the governments of these countries are defeatist, if not actively hostile, towards exporting. Wide fluctuations from year to year in income from key commodity exports harden many politicians in their belief that one prime objective of development is to achieve total economic "independence" from the rest of the world. This desire for economic self-sufficiency runs deep. Since so many export enterprises in the underdeveloped world were the creation of foreign entrepreneurs and are even now owned and operated by foreigners, exporting tends to be regarded as a business for somebody else, if not a reminder of a hated colonial past. At the same time restrictive trade practices and attitudes in the older nations—particularly hostility toward imports of manufactured and semimanufactured goods from the new nations—often discourage governments from channeling investment into new export lines in order to relieve their dependence on one commodity and earn more foreign exchange for their own development.

The trader is in no position to overcome this defeatism and animosity. His concern is naturally for his order book, not for the balance of payments or the political suspicions of the governments in his customers' countries. At the same time the long-term prospects for trade between the West and the underdeveloped countries clearly depend on the capacity and the willingness of the new nations to develop their purchasing power through building up their exports. Therefore the governments of the trading nations in the West, in so far as they are concerned with a rising volume of trade with the new nations, must concern themselves with the export potential of the new nations as well as of their own nations.

Unfortunately all too many of the devices used to promote exports from the industrialized countries reflect no such concern; in fact, they often make matters worse. Loans tied to purchases in the lending country, easy credit terms which run out in a few years and long before the life of the product sold, restrictions against lending for projects in the new nations which might some day provide competition for domestic manufacturers or their exports—all of these devices make the job of creating the right conditions for growth through trade even more difficult. They devalue the aid dollar. But, perhaps most important, they are simply bad business, for in the long run they tend to shrink trade rather than to expand it.

These devices are usually justified on balance-of-payments grounds, and I do not mean to make light of the problem which the industrialized nations face in maintaining external equilibrium. This is a very real problem and one which requires some new and imaginative thought, I believe. But the demands of development diplomacy should be given a hearing in solving this problem. Such a hearing is often lacking now; development aid does not have that separate and distinct status which would allow its contribution to be weighed in the decision.

The future of trade between the West and the underdeveloped world depends primarily on what happens, not in the West, but in the underdeveloped countries. It depends on the kind of balance that is struck in these countries between the desire for autarky and the desire for more rapid growth. The desire for autarky will not be tempered until there is more awareness of how, by underemphasizing exports, the leaders of these nations are prolonging the poverty of their people. This is one of the kinds of choices development diplomacy is supposed to "illuminate." Inasmuch as the future of trade and investment between the West and the underdeveloped world is at stake in this matter, would it not seem wise to grant development diplomacy a chance to do its work?

Economic aid should be a very great help to trade, as is often said. But to be a help, aid must be a means of promoting "the right kinds of decisions" in terms of development, not just a means of rewarding traders. Aid can never be a true substitute for trade—not for the underdeveloped countries, nor for the industrialized countries either.

*   *

It seems clear to me that only by granting development diplomacy a separate status—not an overriding status but a clear and distinct status—in national policy can the stated political and economic interests of the Western nations in the underdeveloped world be served. And, as I have said, if these interests are defined narrowly, it is difficult to see the justification for expanding the scale of aid that is being undertaken now.

But this concept of development diplomacy is sufficiently new and sufficiently radical that it would not be realistic to expect it to gain popular acceptance overnight. Recent history is full of instances where governments develop a rationale for what they are doing only after having done it for quite a while first. I suspect that this is the case with economic aid. The motives behind the West's economic aid programs have tended to metamorphose with the changing course of international politics, and this is hardly surprising in view of the novelty of the challenge with which the West is faced in the underdeveloped world. But as it becomes more obvious that this challenge is in no sense temporary and cannot be "solved" with a bold new program or a universal institution, popular acceptance of development aid as a more or less permanent feature of Western policy can be won. It can be won, I think, if the champions of economic aid allow development diplomacy to be judged on its own merits, not as a means to—at best— dubiously relevant ends.

There are now a variety of programs and institutions— national, international and regional—employing a variety of financial instruments to promote the growth of the new nations. This is as it should be. As a general rule I favor international organization for two reasons: first, it *can* be the easiest way of giving development diplomacy a status separate from conventional diplomacy; second, it *can* be more efficient to pool the resources and the resourcefulness of many nations rather than each nation acting separately. But I recognize that this is not always so and that the principle of a varied approach is necessary and in tune with the realities of this complex world. A variety of programs and institutions poses formidable problems of co-ordination which have not yet been fully realized or investigated. But the diversity of the underdeveloped countries and of their development problems clearly precludes any single formula. I am told that in the heyday of British overseas investment in the last century, there were some fifty separate and distinct kinds of financial institutions operating out of London. The times have not become less complex in the interim.

Likewise, there should be, as there are now, a variety of financial instruments employed in these programs and institutions. Conventional loans alone will not do the job. A developing country can reach very rapidly the prudent limit of its capacity to assume fixed foreign exchange obligations, as we are learning in the Bank. To ignore this prudent limit and simply pile loan upon loan is to destroy the very order in international financial transactions which development diplomacy is in part designed to preserve. This is why we welcomed the initiative of the United States government in suggesting the establishment of an International Development Association, as an affiliate of the World Bank, through which governments can make development capital available for investment on more flexible terms than World Bank loans. We can no longer afford periodic wholesale defaults as a means of cleaning out the international financial system. Instead we have to orchestrate a whole variety of financial instruments, some quite new and novel, if we are to preserve order in the balance of payments of the new nations and to keep in constructive contact with them.

But these are technical points, quite outside my brief. The difference between good development diplomacy and bad development diplomacy is not the difference between a loan and a grant or between an international agency and a national agency; it is the difference between diplomacy which "illuminates the choices" in terms of development and diplomacy which fails to do this. This is a much more useful distinction than it sounds at first. It is now possible to make such a distinction in practice because we have learned a great deal about the choices which governments that wish to force the pace of development must make; it is necessary to have such a distinction, not only to grant development diplomacy its rightful status, but also, as a practical matter, this is the way of figuring the cost of economic aid.

With all the talk about the "need" for economic aid it is often forgotten that it is the congresses and parliaments in the West whose decisions determine what the actual expenditures will be. And congresses and parliaments are not in the habit of supporting vague theories or statistical studies with revenue. They support specific programs and institutions. And in making their decisions congresses and parliaments, responsive to the democratic process, must weigh the benefits and costs of economic aid programs against the benefits and costs of all the other claims, domestic and foreign, on their treasuries. This is a difficult decision at best and the procedures for arriving at a decision are often cumbersome, but no substitute has yet been discovered which is consistent with democracy. In these circumstances, unless development has a separate and distinct status of its own, the congressman or the member of parliament has no rational way of deciding whether too little, too much, or just the right amount is being appropriated for this aim of policy in relation to all the other claims on the taxpayer's dollar.

The champions of economic aid, no less than congresses and parliaments, require a separate and distinct status for their work if they are to exploit fully this new avenue of international co-operation. Even within that big tent called diplomacy they require some room of their own. Economic aid, after all, does not just subsidize people; it influences events. This is so even if the donor simply closes his eyes and gives his money away. Therefore, there is no avoiding the hard job of fashioning programs and institutions through which economic aid can be consciously, deliberately, and effectively administered.

I would suggest that all economic aid programs and institutions be subjected to a simple, but searching test made up of three questions. I would first ask, "Are these institutions and programs illuminating the choices in development which confront the leaders of the underdeveloped world, without the pretense that economic standards of value are somehow morally superior to other standards of value?" Then I would ask, "Are they making and maintaining constructive contacts, working partnerships that promise to remain working even in the face of the controversies which bedevil conventional diplomacy today?" And finally, "Can these institutions and programs point to visible results in terms of engineering a series of escapes from poverty?"

I suggest that it is, to borrow a phrase from the economists, the "absorptive capacity" of institutions and programs which pass this test that is the practical measure of the effective—and justifiable—demand for economic aid at any given time. If this is not a neat way to measure the "need" for economic aid, it is, I think, the only realistic way. It meets the requirements of orderly democratic processes in the West and provides a rational basis for judging the degree of sacrifice which the Western nations should be willing to make in order to influence the course of the so-called revolution of rising expectations.

One way or another, the Western nations will have to live intimately with the historic transformation going on in the underdeveloped world. The question is, will these nations also live constructively with that transformation or will they merely seek to insulate themselves from the effects of historical forces which they themselves are so largely responsible for having loosed? Development diplomacy is one logical means to a hopeful modus vivendi; there may in fact be no other means that is both so logical and so hopeful.

The promise of development diplomacy rests on the assumption that the ultimate test of a free society is its ability to survive, not as a museum piece in an alien and hostile world, but as a dynamic society, continually absorbed in working partnerships with other nations and other peoples. This is not to equate material progress with human progress. On the contrary, development diplomacy gets its justification from a more realistic view, which sees human progress as an endless series of escapes from one human predicament to another with the ground of hope the measure of advance. This is why I think it commends itself in a part of the world where the balance of hope is more of an issue than the balance of power.

But development diplomacy cannot succeed without a new sense of vocation in the West, one which takes into itself the hard realities of the world as it is, yet reflects a courageous belief in a future compatible with liberty and tolerance. A means of expressing such a vocation lies readily at hand in the opportunity to combat the oppressive poverty of the new nations of the world. I feel sure that over time the West will seize more and more of this opportunity. For it is rare in international affairs that doing the obvious makes so much sense.

APPENDIX

A NOTE ON THE WORLD BANK*

When the International Bank for Reconstruction and Development (usually called the World Bank) informed its members in June 1946 that it was ready to begin operations, nothing quite like this new intergovernmental association had ever existed. Its Articles of Agreement stated its mission: to assist in the reconstruction and development of its member countries by stimulating the international investment of capital for productive purposes. The Bank was to guarantee loans made for these purposes. It could itself make loans out of capital or borrowed funds, but only if other investors were unwilling to lend on reasonable terms.

For operating policies and methods, the Articles offered guide lines, not specifications. Written large in the charter, nevertheless, was the intent to keep the new institution clear of the reefs onto which the Great Depression had driven some of the more extravagant loans of the 1920's. Whether as guarantor or lender, the Bank was required to make a prudent assessment of the prospects that loans would be repaid. Normally, it was to associate itself with the financing of specific projects. It was expected to study and choose those projects for their usefulness and urgency to the country concerned; and it was required to exercise any care necessary to insure that loans were applied effectively to the purposes for which they were made. With allowance for special circumstances, the Bank was to guarantee or make loans in foreign exchange rather than in the domestic currency of the borrower.

* Prepared by the staff of the International Bank for Reconstruction and Development.

61

The role of the Bank was to be marginal—marginal to private international investment, and marginal to domestic investment in the member countries themselves. Within that scope, the charter left ample room in which the Bank could grow. The Articles contained admonitions, but few prohibitions; and the emphasis of the charter was at least as much on what the new institution should do as on what it should not.

*   *   *

The Bank opened its doors, nearly a year after the end of the war, on a world still in crisis. The peace had not been secured: alarms of war were, in fact, to persist for more than a decade. An international program for the relief and rehabilitation of war-devastated countries was coming to an end and, while massive United States aid was being provided, it was not certain how much longer this aid would continue.

There was no question of meeting Europe's needs by private international investment. The Bank itself had to lend. Yet it could not lend hastily, for in 1946 it was watching the deepening international economic crisis with only about $700 million of usable funds in sight. It had not yet tested its ability to raise capital by borrowing. It had no earnings, no reserves, and, for that matter, no operating experience as an institution.

The Bank, nevertheless, had been established to take risks. From May into August 1947, it made $497 million of reconstruction loans in four countries of Western Europe: France, the Netherlands, Denmark, and Luxembourg. The timing of these loans was crucial: coming from seven months to a year before the Marshall Plan, they helped maintain a flow of essential imports when an interruption would have been a serious setback to European recovery.

With the adoption of the Marshall Plan by the United States in April 1948, the Bank was able to turn from the emergency of reconstruction to its long-term task: assistance in the economic development of its member countries. It continued to lend in Europe, but it now also began to deal actively with the less-developed countries elsewhere. The Bank's first loans in these countries were in Latin America; two loans were made in Chile in 1948. The Bank's first loan in Asia (to India) was made in 1949; its first loans to Australia, and its first lending in Africa (to Ethiopia) and in the Middle East (to Iraq) came in 1950.

In most of these areas, the Bank found itself faced with problems very different from those of European reconstruction. Here the task was not simply to restore missing components to economies already mature; it was to strengthen foundations. A dearth of basic services was (and still is) the major physical obstacle to increasing production and raising living standards in the less developed countries. Lack of these services put severe limits on productivity, on income, and on the willingness to invest. The lack of dependable and economical transportation restricted the size of markets for both industrial and agricultural production, and kept regions with promising natural resources beyond the reach of development. Deficiencies of electric power supply conspicuously handicapped industrial growth.

To strengthen basic services and so to set free new productive energies has been the main objective of the Bank's development lending from the outset. The Bank has made more development loans to develop electric power than for any other purpose; but it has lent nearly as much for highways, railways, ports, and other means of transportation. Taken together, power and transportation account for two thirds of the Bank's development lending. Projects in these fields have plainly met the Bank's tests of usefulness and urgency; and, in general, private capital has not been available for projects of this type, even when they were revenue-producing. For the rest, the Bank's loans have been made for industry, agriculture, or programs involving several sectors of the economy at the same time.

At first, the Bank's development lending was slow to gather momentum. It rose gradually to an annual rate of $300 million beginning in the fiscal year 1951, then to $400 million a year beginning in 1954. Beginning in 1958, however, the rate rose suddenly to $700 million a year, and this pace has been maintained. By mid-1960, the gross total of the Bank's loans (including its reconstruction lending) had risen to over $5 billion, consisting of 260 loans for governmental or private projects in 52 countries and territories. Actual disbursements rose correspondingly: in calender 1958, they amounted to one tenth of the international flow of capital to the low-income countries from all sources, and accounted for one fourth of the flow from public sources.

To enable the Bank to meet the rising demand for development loans, member governments increased its authorized capital from the equivalent of $10 billion to $21 billion in 1959. In the meantime, proposals already had been made to increase the Bank's usefulness further by creating new institutions as affiliates to it. One of these, the International Finance Corporation, was established with an authorized capital of $100 million in 1956 to make investments in private enterprises, especially in underdeveloped areas. The IFC has concentrated on aid to industrial ventures; unlike the Bank, it is able to invest in private undertakings without governmental guarantee, and is able to make investments other than fixed-interest loans. In 1960, the sixty-eight member governments of the Bank were taking legislative action on a second proposal, to create an International Development Association, administered by the Bank but able to make loans on easier terms of repayment. According to the proposed Articles of Agreement, IDA would have an authorized capital equivalent to $1 billion, and would come into being by the end of 1960.

* * *

Once the Bank moved from reconstruction into development lending, the guide lines of the Articles were only the beginnings of paths into new territory. Moving carefully from problem to specific problem, the Bank had to elaborate its own policies and mark out its own trails. In the underdeveloped world, the need for outside capital was pressing, but so was the need for creating the conditions and supplying the skills necessary for using capital more effectively than it had been used in the past.

The Articles had enjoined the Bank to insure that its funds were economically and efficiently used. In consequence, the Bank has wished to be satisfied that the economic benefits expected from a project proposed for financing have been properly evaluated, that the project is well designed for the function it is to perform, that the engineering plans have been completely drawn, that cost estimates are complete and realistic, that funds will in fact be available to cover expenditures not financed by the Bank's loan, and that the borrower has made adequate managerial and administrative arrangements, not only for building the project but for operating it once construction has been completed.

It was inevitable that many proposals made to the Bank should be incomplete in these respects. For the underdeveloped countries had relatively few leaders in business or government able to plan investment; and they were greatly hampered by a shortage of technicians and managers able to design and carry out development projects. In these circumstances, it seemed plain that the Bank could not simply accept or reject loan proposals. If it were to help finance any considerable number

65

of projects, it would have to offer advice about how to prepare them as well.

The Bank therefore not only closely examined what was proposed, through studies of documentation and visits to the field. It also developed the practice of suggesting modifications or further study whenever necessary. It quickly found itself playing—and has since continued to play—an advisory role of considerable scope and variety, concerned with economics, engineering, organization and many other factors bearing on the eventual success of the project.

Nor does the signing of a loan contract end the matter, for the Articles require the Bank to see that loans are actually spent for the purposes intended. The Bank, accordingly, has asked its borrowers for regular reports of progress made, and periodically sends its staff to examine progress at first hand. The measures taken by the Bank to follow its loans have frequently made it possible to help the borrower to move promptly toward a solution of unexpected difficulties. As the number and variety of proposals presented to it have increased, the Bank has steadily had to add to its staff of specialists particularly concerned with the assessment and execution of projects; and a separate department was established in 1952 to be responsible for project appraisal and for advising borrowers on project problems.

*　　*　　*

The Bank, however, could not logically confine—and has never confined—its attention to the accomplishment of particular projects. For the Bank's financing of economic development could never be more than marginal to investment from other sources. The Bank could not hope that its loans would stimulate private investment in a member country whose policies discouraged that kind of investment. Nor could the Bank look only to the results of individual projects for the repayment of its loan; that would depend, in the last analysis, on the whole economy and especially on the availability of foreign exchange resources.

For these reasons, among others, the Bank from the beginning of its operations has been interested in questions that go beyond the particular project proposed for financing. One of these questions is whether the project itself, judged against the needs of the economy as a whole, promises enough return to justify borrowing on the scale suggested; another is whether the necessary complements to the project exist in the economy —whether farm mechanization, for instance, would be frustrated for want of roads able to carry new produce to market.

The Bank has been at least equally concerned with the economic environment in which its loans are to be put to work. In loan discussions, it has as a matter of course consistently urged attempts to settle defaulted external debt, to put economic and fiscal policies on a sound footing, and to direct public investment in such a way as to promote, rather than to obstruct or displace, the flow of private capital.

The most comprehensive instrument for giving developmental advice to member countries, however, is the general survey mission. The first of these missions was organized in 1949, in response to a request from the government of Colombia for a thorough analysis of the Colombian economy and for recommendations on which the government could base the formulation of a long-term program for economic development. In all, the Bank has now organized almost a score of general survey missions to its member countries, and has engaged in a number of other undertakings analogous to these missions and in some cases deriving their inspiration from them—specialized studies, for instance, of agricultural development in Uruguay, Chile, and Colombia. The general survey mission has also been the forerunner of other forms of developmental assistance, especially of the maintenance of resident

representatives in selected member countries to assist governments in the programming and execution of measures for
economic development. A further and logical outcome of the
Bank's interest in the formulation of development policies was
the establishment in 1955 of an Economic Development Insti-
tute as a staff college for senior officials, with the objective of
improving the management of economic affairs in the less
developed countries.

* * *

The Bank's lending activities are spread over six continents.
To finance its lending, the Bank has marshalled funds on a
scale hardly less world-wide.

The Bank at first had only dollars to lend—and, indeed, in
the period of European reconstruction, most of the goods its
borrowers wanted could be purchased only for dollars. In
April 1947, the United States freed for lending all of the paid-
in part of its subscription to the Bank's capital. Soon after,
Canada began to release its paid-in subscription, and by 1952
all the Canadian dollars originally subscribed to the Bank had
been made available for loans.

In the meantime, economic recovery was creating conditions
in which European countries could once more begin to send
capital and capital goods abroad. From 1952 onward, the
Bank was able to allocate increasing amounts of European
currencies for lending. By 1959, virtually all the Western
European currencies held by the Bank had been freed for
lending, and countries in other parts of the world had also
begun to release appreciable amounts of their own capital sub-
scriptions for lending. By the end of 1959, the Bank had been
able to make loans in thirty-two different currencies.

The Bank was never intended, however, simply to deploy
funds subscribed by governments; it was to play a larger role
in bringing about the international investment of capital from

other sources. The only capital market able to provide funds, in the Bank's first year of operations, was the United States. Two months after the first reconstruction loan, the Bank successfully sold a $250 million issue of bonds in the United States market. In mid-1960 a billion dollars of the Bank's bonds, distributed among fourteen different issues, are in the hands of American investors.

The Bank early explored other markets. Bonds denominated in Swiss francs were placed privately in Switzerland as soon as 1948; the first public issue outside the United States was floated for pounds sterling in the United Kingdom in 1951. In the meantime, parts of the Bank's United States dollar issues had begun to be sold abroad; by 1960, the Bank had sold four entire dollar issues outside the United States. Sales on bonds in currencies other than U.S. dollars continued; the Bank entered the markets of Belgium, Canada, Germany, and the Netherlands with public issues. The Bank's bonds and notes are now held in more than forty countries, and investors outside the United States hold more than a billion dollars' worth, amounting to more than half of all the Bank's borrowings.

The Bank has enlisted the help of the investment market in two other important ways. The first is the sale of Bank loans to other investors, either at the time a loan is made or at any time thereafter. These sales aggregated about $800 million by mid-1960, and to that extent had enabled the Bank to revolve its resources and provide funds for new lending. The other technique is the joint Bank-market operation whereby member countries are introduced to the bond market as borrowers on their own account. This technique is appropriate with the more developed member countries which are able to stand on their own feet as borrowers. The procedure is for the Bank to make a loan to a particular country to coincide with the sale of that country's bonds on the investment market in the United States. The reputation of the Bank increases investor confidence and facilitates the sale of the borrower's bonds. Once introduced to the market, the borrower may thereafter be able to enter in on his own account. Examples of this system in action comprise ten countries of Europe, Africa, and Asia. The more this technique can be used, the more the private investment market can resume its position as the principal financier of development, leaving the Bank's funds for use in the less developed countries which cannot for the time being borrow on long term through normal commercial channels.

*   *   *

The Bank's international character, its reputation for objectivity and its expertness in finance led it logically but unexpectedly into the field of international mediation. The first such venture actually to be undertaken was an attempt by the Bank's management in February-March 1952 to find a caretaker basis on which the operation of the Iranian oil fields could be resumed, pending an agreement between the Government of Iran and the Anglo-Iranian Oil Company. In 1958, mediation by the management of the Bank successfully brought to settlement claims and counterclaims, arising out of the nationalization of the Suez Canal, between the Government of the United Arab Republic and the shareholders of the Suez Canal company. Early in the following year, the President of the Bank was able to help the Governments of the United Arab Republic and of the United Kingdom to reach agreement on a settlement of the financial claims which arose out of the Suez incident of 1956.

Looming over all these matters were the efforts of the Bank's management to resolve a dispute directly affecting the livelihood of 40 million people on the Indian subcontinent. Late in 1951, the Bank proffered its good offices to help the

Governments of India and Pakistan to evolve a plan for sharing and developing the waters of the Indus River system. The Bank's offer was accepted in March 1952, and work looking toward agreement on a comprehensive scheme was begun that summer. After it became apparent that the respective plans of the two governments could not be reconciled, the Bank put forward a plan of its own in February 1954. Negotiations were subsequently carried on in Karachi, New Delhi, and London, as well as Washington, and culminated in the signing of an Indus Waters Treaty at Karachi in September 1960. In the meantime the Bank had been able to make arrangements for an Indus River Development Fund, whereby the Bank and six "friendly governments" would provide the bulk of the finance needed to carry out the development of the Indus River system; and the international agreement establishing the Fund was signed at the same time as the Treaty.

*   *   *

In mid-1960, the Bank had been one of many participants in fifteen eventful years of efforts to raise standards of living in the underdeveloped countries of the world. The Bank had affected, and been affected by, the international development effort; it had been driven, and had driven itself, to a variety of activity not imagined by its founders. As an international organization, it was privileged to have an unusually wide opportunity to gain experience; it also had the opportunity to apply that experience in a practical and effective way to the problems of a world membership. Of it, a friendly and well-informed observer wrote, "The Bank has shown itself capable of adapting itself to changing circumstances: of altering its methods of operation and starting fresh experiments in international organization. . . . It retains the idealism and enterprise with which it started and has succeeded in mixing this with hard-headedness and thoroughness. Few international organizations have maintained so lively an atmosphere or one so favorable to the purposes for which they were established."

Index

73